CENGAGE Learning

Shakespeare for Students, Second Edition, Volume 1

Project Editor
Anne Marie Hacht

Rights Acquisition and Management
Lisa Kincade, Robbie McCord, Lista Person, Kelly Quin, and Andrew Specht

Manufacturing
Rita Wimberley

Imaging
Lezlie Light

Product Design
Pamela A. E. Galbreath and Jennifer Wahi

Vendor Administration
Civie Green

Product Manager
Meggin Condino

© 2007 Gale, a part of Cengage Learning Inc.

Cengage and Burst Logo are trademarks and Gale is a registered trademark used herein under license.

For more information, contact
Gale, an imprint of Cengage Learning
27500 Drake Rd.
Farmington Hills, MI 48331-3535
Or you can visit our Internet site at http://www.gale.com

ALL RIGHTS RESERVED
No part of this work covered by the copyright hereon may be reproduced or used in any form or by any means—graphic, electronic, or mechanical, including photocopying, recording, taping, Web distribution, or information storage retrieval systems—without the written permission of the publisher.

For permission to use material from this product, submit your request via Web at http://www.gale-edit.com/permissions, or you may download our Permissions Request form and submit your request by fax or mail to:

Permissions Department
Gale, an imprint of Cengage Learning
27500 Drake Rd.
Farmington Hills, MI 48331-3535
Permissions Hotline: 248-699-8006 or 800-877-4253, ext. 8006
Fax: 248-699-8074 or 800-762-4058

Since this page cannot legibly accommodate all copyright notices, the acknowledgments constitute an extension of the copyright notice.

While every effort has been made to ensure the reliability of the information presented in this publication, Gale, an imprint of Cengage Learning does not guarantee the accuracy of the data contained herein. Gale, an imprint of Cengage Learning accepts no payment for listing; and inclusion in the publication of any organization, agency, institution, publication, service, or individual does not imply endorsement of the editors or publisher. Errors brought to the attention of the publisher and verified to the satisfaction of the publisher will be corrected in future editions.

LIBRARY OF CONGRESS CATALOGING-IN-PUBLICATION DATA

Shakespeare for students: critical interpretations of Shakespeare's plays and poetry.-2nd ed. / Anne Marie Hacht, editor; foreword by Cynthia Burnstein.

p. cm.

Includes bibliographical references and index.

ISBN-13: 978-1-4144-1255-9 (set)
ISBN-10: 1-4144-1255-X (set)
ISBN-13: 978-1-4144-1256-6 (v. 1)
ISBN-10: 1-4144-1256-8 (v. 1)
[etc.]

1. Shakespeare, William, 1564–1616—Outlines, syllabi, *etc.* 2. Shakespeare, William, 1564–1616—Criticism and interpretation. 3. Shakespeare, William, 1564–1616—Examinations-Study guides. I. Hacht, Anne Marie.

PR2987.S47 2007

822.3'3—dc22 2007008901

ISBN-13
978-1-4144-1255-9 (set)
978-1-4144-1256-6 (vol. 1)
978-1-4144-1258-0 (vol. 2)
978-1-4144-1259-7 (vol. 3)

ISBN-10
1-1444-1255-X (set)
1-4144-1256-8 (vol. 1)
1-4144-1258-4 (vol. 2)
1-4144-1259-2 (vol. 3)

This title is also available as an e-book.
ISBN-13 978-1-4144-2937-3 (set) ISBN-10 1-4144-2937-1 (set)
Contact your Gale, an imprint of Cengage Learning sales representative for ordering information.

Printed in the United States of America

10 9 8 7 6 5 4 3 2 1

As You Like It

William Shakespeare
1599

Introduction

Commentators have described the comedy *As You Like It* as both a celebration of the spirit of pastoral romance and a satire of the pastoral ideal, where the term *pastoral* refers to the simple, innocent life of the countryside. Audiences usually prefer the light-hearted, love-oriented banter and whimsy that dominate the scenes in the Forest of Arden to the sorrowful, battle-filled atmospheres at the home of Oliver and the court of Duke Frederick. The forest is conceivably a reference to both the Arden woodlands near Shakespeare's hometown and the region of Ardennes, in northeast France, where

Shakespeare sets the action of the play. In its tranquility the forest enchants the visitors, who, after securing nourishment and shelter, think of little but love during their wanderings. The non-romantic plot threads established in the first act essentially resolve themselves in the final scenes, in large part because the forest seems to also enchant the antagonists as soon as they arrive. The play's naturally magical aspect is made tangible when Hymen, the Greek god of marriage, appears to officiate at the weddings that close the play.

The final three acts, then, give the audience a chance to feel how "Time ambles" (3.2.305) for those with plenty of leisure and no obligations, as is the case with the main characters. Although Rosalind presumably needs to disguise herself to ensure her safety, nothing actually threatens her union with Orlando; the two are mutually infatuated from their first meeting. Thus, most of the tension in the play, with the original plot threads picked up only during the scene at the duke's palace at the beginning of the third act, stems from the various witty exchanges. Touchstone and Jaques contribute to the play not through love affairs—the former woos Audrey only halfheartedly, while the latter seems incapable of love—but through philosophical reflection, which the solitude of the pastoral setting encourages.

Shakespeare derived the plot of *As You Like It* directly from the novel *Rosalynde, or Euphues' Golden Legacy*, published in 1590 by Thomas Lodge. (Copyright protection did not exist in the

Elizabethan era.) Lodge's novel in turn was based on a more action-oriented fourteenth-century poem entitled "The Tale of Gamelyn." While veering little from Lodge's straightforward pastoral tale, Shakespeare did strengthen the character of Rosalind and add his two philosophers, Jaques and Touchstone, providing the opportunity for greater reflection among the cast as a whole.

Although critics remain divided on whether *As You Like It* should be read as a satire or a celebration of the pastoral ideal, readers can take pleasure in the play's festive atmosphere and its various love affairs. *As You Like It* is one of Shakespeare's most popular and best-loved comedies.

Plot Summary

Act 1, Scene 1

In the opening scene of *As You Like It*, Orlando tells the old family servant Adam of his discontent with his brother Oliver's management of the family fortune and his treatment of him, for he is being allowed no education and thus will have no means to advance in the world. This speech, with Orlando's referring to "the spirit of my father, which I think is within me" (21-2), introduces a filial connection that establishes Orlando as the novel's hero in both a romantic and a moral sense. When Oliver arrives, Orlando bests him first with wit, then with strength, ultimately demanding the share that their deceased father had allotted to him. Oliver placates Orlando, then curses Adam, who reveals his fond remembrance of their father, Sir Rowland de Boys, and effectively allies himself with Orlando.

Left alone, Oliver summons the court wrestler, Charles, who provides an account of the state of the ducal court (largely for the audience, in that he is only delivering "old news" (96-7): the elder Duke Senior has been ousted and banished by his younger brother Frederick. Rosalind, the daughter of the banished Duke Senior, has remained at the court only because she is highly favored by her cousin Celia. Meanwhile, Duke Senior and the lords who joined him in exile have settled in the evidently idyllic Forest of Arden, where they "fleet the time carelessly, as they did in the golden world" (114-15). As Charles will be wrestling a disguised Orlando the following day, Oliver entreats him to do as much harm as possible. Oliver's scene-closing monologue leaves no doubt about his role as a villain: he despises Orlando solely because the youngest of the three brothers is so benevolent and beloved.

Act 1, Scene 2

Upon their first appearance in the play, Rosalind mourns the absence of her father while Celia tries to persuade her to content herself with the friendship they share. Rosalind suggests that falling in love might distract her from her sorrows, and Celia agrees that she could "make sport withal" (25), which she will indeed do, but cautions against loving "in good earnest" (26), which she will also do. After ruminating on the goddesses Fortune and Nature, the two women greet Touchstone, the court fool, who marks his entrance with a trivial display of wit regarding knightly honor. The courtier Monsieur Le Beau then arrives to inform the three of the wrestling match about to take place there.

When Duke Frederick enters—accompanied by a shift from prose to blank verse, which endows the action with greater gravity until the end of the scene—he entreats the ladies to persuade the young challenger to stand down. When they cannot refute Orlando's tragically heroic reasons for fighting—no one would truly regret the loss of his life anyway, and he wishes to test himself—he proceeds to defeat the champion, Charles, to Rosalind's cry of "Hercules be thy speed, young man!" (199). In turn, Frederick expresses disappointment, because he was an enemy of Orlando's father—while Rosalind's father, Duke Senior, had held Sir Rowland de Boys in the highest esteem. The ladies commend Orlando, with Rosalind dramatically giving him a chain from around her neck, before exiting, leaving Orlando dumbfounded by his growing passion for Rosalind. Le Beau then returns, first warning Orlando that he ought to leave the dukedom, as he has aroused Frederick's displeasure, then informing Orlando about the identities of Rosalind and Celia.

Act 1, Scene 3

Rosalind discusses her adoration for Orlando with Celia, exchanging a fair amount of wit and referring to him as potentially being her "child's father" (11). Duke Frederick, however, interrupts the scene—to the return of blank verse—to banish Rosalind, citing a general mistrust of her intentions; also, just as Oliver dislikes Orlando for his virtue, Frederick takes issue with the fact that "Her very silence, and her patience, / Speak to the people, and they pity her" (76-7). Frederick also tries to convince his daughter that she would be better off without her cousin as a rival. The two women then decide to journey to the Forest of Arden disguised as peasants, with the taller Rosalind posing as a man named Ganymede and Celia posing as a woman named Aliena; gathering the clown Touchstone and their "jewels" and "wealth" (132), they depart.

Act 2, Scene 1

The second act provides a transition from the court to the forest, with the first scene taking place in Arden, the second at court, the third at Oliver's, and each scene thereafter in the forest. The foremost patriarchal figure of the woodlands is introduced, Duke Senior, who is attended by Amiens and a number of lords. After extolling upon the virtues of the forest, Duke Senior regrets his company's need to kill the deer, who are true forest natives, for their meat. One lord mentions how the "melancholy Jaques" (26, 41), who was just seen mourning a mortally wounded deer, is particularly revolted by their intrusions on nature. Interested in some conversation with the philosophizer—if only for amusement—Duke Senior and his lords depart in search of him.

Act 2, Scene 2

At the court, briefly, Duke Frederick is made aware of the disappearance of both his niece and his daughter and also of their expressed affection for Orlando, who may have accompanied them. Frederick then summons Oliver.

Act 2, Scene 3

At Oliver's house, Adam meets Orlando and

praises his many virtues, affectionately referring to him as a "memory / of old Sir Rowland" (2-3), then warns him that Oliver is scheming to have him murdered, if not by arson then by some other means. Knowing he would be unable to live life as an amoral thief, Orlando resolves to face his brother —until Adam volunteers his life's savings and his service to help the youngest brother find shelter and provisions somewhere. The two depart together.

Act 2, Scene 4

Rosalind, Celia, and Touchstone appear in the Forest of Arden, incredibly weary from their travels, with the fool regretting having left the court. The woodland shepherds Corin and Silvius then appear, softening the mood of the scene by speaking of love: Silvius expresses his adoration of Phebe and accuses the elder Corin of having never been a true lover himself, as he remembers none of his lover's follies. Rosalind is reminded of her own aching for Orlando, and Touchstone reminisces somewhat soberly upon a love of his youth. The fool then calls out to Corin, and Rosalind inquires about lodgings and food; through Corin, they secure the purchase of a cottage and a flock of sheep.

Act 2, Scene 5

Amiens and Jaques share songs about the peacefulness of the forest, where the only enemies are "winter and rough weather" (7). Jaques again mentions his distaste for men, specifically their general lack of manners, and notes that he has been avoiding Duke Senior because he finds him "too disputable" (31).

Act 2, Scene 6

Adam and Orlando stumble into the Forest of Arden. When Adam collapses, Orlando sets out to seek help for him.

Act 2, Scene 7

Jaques and Duke Senior meet, and Jaques relates his earlier encounter with Touchstone when the fool uttered some witty comments about the passing of the time. Duke Senior scoffs at the soundness of Jaques's judgments given his checkered past. Orlando then arrives, threatening to attack them and rob them of their food, only to be offered the food gladly by the gentlemanly Duke Senior. As Orlando leaves to return to Adam, Duke Senior and Jaques muse on the theatricality of life, with Jaques giving the famous "seven ages" speech, in which he remarks that a single man goes through seven stages, or acts, in the course of his lifetime. ("All the world's a stage / And all the men and women merely players.") Amiens marks the meal with a song, "Blow, blow, thou winter wind," and the duke rejoices in meeting the son of his beloved and deceased friend Sir Rowland de Boys.

Act 3, Scene 1

At his palace, Duke Frederick orders Oliver to bring his brother to the court within a year or be exiled himself. As Oliver grovels, Duke Frederick scorns him as a villain for having never loved his own brother.

Act 3, Scene 2

Orlando hangs love poems to Rosalind on trees throughout the forest, singing her praises as he does so. With the entrance of the fool and a shepherd, the play reverts to prose form; Touchstone demands that the shepherd Corin give an acceptable accounting of why he should spend his life in the countryside rather than at court. The fool manages to phrase his own reasons for favoring the court with enough nuance to stymie the peasant. Rosalind interrupts them as she arrives reading one of the anonymous poems written about her, which Touchstone promptly ridicules as being pedantic and dull, devising his own pithy and mocking rhymes. Celia then arrives reading a somewhat longer poem that Rosalind finds tedious.

The two women send the two men off so they can talk together. Rosalind begins by deriding the author's poetic abilities. Celia then reveals to her cousin that she saw the poet hanging up one of the sheets—and that he wears Rosalind's chain around his neck, at which news Rosalind reddens but seems not to realize that the man is Orlando. Celia first describes him, then reveals his identity, and Rosalind becomes quite agitated by romantic sentiments.

Orlando himself then appears on the scene, chatting with Jaques, and the women hide. Orlando relates his affections for Rosalind and responds to Jaques's probing inquiries with fine wit. When Jaques slinks off, Rosalind disguised as Ganymede approaches, intending to best Orlando in conversation. She ends up carrying on a profound discourse about the passage of time experienced by people who spend their time differently. From the beginning, the conversation is strained by Rosalind's attempts to conceal her person. After remarking on how glad she is not to be a woman, Rosalind belittles Orlando for allowing himself to be infected with love, which she sees evidenced by his poems more than by his person. Rosalind then remarks that she can cure Orlando of his love if he will focus his affection on her (that is to say, Ganymede), and substitute the name *Rosalind* instead. He is skeptical but he agrees, and they head for the women's cottage.

Act 3, Scene 3

In the forest, Touchstone and Audrey are carrying on something of a courtship, while Jaques watches from a concealed location. Audrey reveals her unfamiliarity with the notion of the "poetical" (15), while Touchstone flaunts his wit and makes little secret of his desire simply to have sexual relations with the female goatherd. After mentioning that he has brought along a local vicar to perform a marriage ceremony to legitimate their lovemaking, he speaks at length about animals and men and their horns, sustaining the sexual references. When Sir Oliver Mar-text begins to conduct the wedding, Jaques offers to give away the bride and then convinces Touchstone that such a dull marriage would not befit the gentleman that he is. Jaques at last leads the couple away.

Act 3, Scene 4

At their cottage in the morning, Rosalind anxiously awaits Orlando, fretting to Celia about the color of his hair while admiring his evident chasteness. Celia admits that she doubts the truth of his love, leading Rosalind to inquire further. Rosalind also mentions that she met her father the day before and successfully maintained her disguise. When Corin arrives to lead them to the spectacle of Silvius trying to court Phebe (at which point the text switches to blank verse, the first time that such a change is introduced for a peasant) Rosalind remarks that she may "prove a busy actor in their play" (56).

Act 3, Scene 5

As Silvius begs Phebe to show him but the smallest kindness, Rosalind, Celia, and Corin arrive to observe. Phebe rejects Silvius saying that no man should be truly hurt by emotional disappointment. As Silvius despairs, Rosalind enters to first make fun of Phebe's appearance and then suggest to

Silvius that he would be better off seeking another mate; ultimately she recommends that they form a union, even if it might produce "ill-favored children" (53). However, Phebe takes an instant liking to Ganymede, despite, if not because of, his aggressiveness. When Silvius and Phebe are again left alone, Phebe agrees to love Silvius not romantically but as a neighbor, as we0ll as to employ him. Subsequently, she inquires about Ganymede and expresses how appealing she found his softer qualities. At last recalling Ganymede's bitterness and claiming to be offended by him, Phebe entreats Silvius to bring Ganymede a letter that she will compose.

Act 4, Scene 1

Jaques is engaging in conversation with the disguised Rosalind and Celia, offering justification for his melancholy, which he claims stems in part from his travels; Rosalind says that she prefers the amusement of a fool to the sadness fostered by experience. When Orlando appears, Jaques exits, leaving Rosalind to chide Orlando for being so late to a meeting with one he supposedly loves. After comparing him unfavorably to a snail, which at least has a home and horns on its head, Rosalind then urges Orlando to try and woo her. They banter about kissing and chasteness, then Rosalind echoes Phebe's earlier remarks about no man having ever truly died from love.

When Orlando objects to Rosalind's lamenting

tone, she becomes pleasanter, and they engage in a mock wedding ceremony. Nevertheless, she again grows negative, offering a list of ways in which she would disappoint Orlando as a wife. Ultimately she asserts that above all she would not abandon her wit, and if her husband tried to dismiss her, she would simply turn to another man. Orlando then departs to join the duke at dinner, asserting that he will return in two hours, and Rosalind remarks that if he breaks that promise, he will be thoroughly out of favor. Celia then chastises Rosalind for her disparaging remarks about the female sex, to which Rosalind replies only by celebrating the depth of her love for Orlando.

Act 4, Scene 2

Jaques and a few lords are found celebrating their successful deer hunt, although Jaques had earlier mourned the death of a hunted deer. One of the lords offers a song ritualizing the wearing of the deer's horns, horns that are portrayed as almost sacred.

Act 4, Scene 3

As Celia and Rosalind wonder about Orlando's failure to return on time, Silvius appears—accompanied by blank verse—to present Rosalind, still dressed as Ganymede, with a supposedly caustic letter from Phebe. In fact, finding the message to be one of love, Rosalind seizes the opportunity to jest with Silvius: she first claims that some man, certainly he, must have in fact written the "giant-rude" (35) invective therein, then reads the letter aloud to reveal its actual loving contents. Finally, she sends Silvius on his way, although he is hopelessly in love with Phebe.

Oliver then arrives in search of the cottage and the disguised women, bearing a handkerchief stained with blood. He relates how Orlando had happened upon a man sleeping under a tree with a snake wrapped about his neck and a lioness crouching in the bushes nearby. The snake slithered away, leaving Orlando to discover that the man was none other than his elder brother Oliver; after some indecision, Orlando drove off the lioness, saving Oliver's life. Upon reaching the safety of the realm of Duke Senior, Orlando collapsed from a wound he received, then entreated Oliver to bring the handkerchief to Rosalind as a token. At this news, Rosalind herself swoons, leaving Oliver somewhat unconvinced of her masculinity. She hopes that Oliver will tell Orlando that she had only pretended to faint.

Act 5, Scene 1

Audrey and Touchstone are conversing, with Audrey regretting that they had not been married earlier by the adequate priest. Audrey then confirms that William "lays claim to" (7) but has "no interest in" (8) her, and Touchstone prepares to belittle him with wit. After conversing inconsequentially, the fool concludes by threatening the hapless William with death if he should try to maintain relations with Audrey.

Act 5, Scene 2

Oliver discusses his newfound adoration for Celia (as Aliena) with Orlando, also telling his younger brother that he intends to remain in the forest and live the life of a humble shepherd; if he does, Orlando will inherit their father's estate. Upon Rosalind's arrival, Orlando—who refers to the "greater wonders" (27) related to him by his brother and may thus be aware of Rosalind's disguise—rues the fact that his brother gets to enjoy his love in the present. Orlando states that he "can live no longer by thinking," that is, about his absent love (50). Rosalind, as Ganymede, then relates how she has long "conversed with a magician" (60-1) and promises that she will bring the true Rosalind the following day.

Silvius and Phebe then arrive, with Silvius professing his love for her, while she professes her love for Ganymede—and Orlando once more professes his love for Rosalind. Rosalind then promises to resolve all of their conflicts of love the following day, presenting the intended outcome in such a witty way that everyone is content.

Act 5, Scene 3

Touchstone and Audrey look forward to their coming wedding, with two of Duke Senior's pages arriving and singing the company a song about love and springtime. Touchstone concludes their tune with some sardonic remarks about the time he just wasted.

Act 5, Scene 4

In the closing scene, Duke Senior, Jaques, Orlando, Oliver, Silvius, Phebe, Celia, and Rosalind are gathered, with Rosalind receiving confirmation from everyone that they will agree to the various proposed unions. The two disguised women then leave, with Duke Senior and Orlando commenting upon Ganymede's resemblance to Rosalind.

Media Adaptations

- Among a number of motion picture versions of *As You Like It*, one of the most notable was produced by International Allied in 1936, directed by Paul Czinner. It features the renowned Laurence Olivier as Orlando in his first Shakespeare role on film, as well as Elisabeth Bergner playing Rosalind.

- An educational video entitled *"As You Like It": An Introduction* was produced by BHE Education in 1969, offering performances of key scenes from the comedy, accompanied by brief instructional narratives.

- A television adaptation of *As You Like It* was produced by the British Broadcasting Corporation in 1979, as distributed by Time-Life Video. It was directed by Brian Coleman and stars Helen Mirren as Rosalind.

- Kenneth Branagh directed a film version of *As You Like It* that was released in 2006, as produced by Picturehouse, featuring such renowned stars as Bryce Dallas Howard (Rosalind), Kevin Kline (Jaques), and Alfred Molina (Touchstone).

Touchstone and Audrey then arrive, with Jaques praising the fool's wit. Touchstone frames his acceptance of Audrey as a noble deed, then goes on to relate a quarrel he had, naming all of the retorts and reproofs according to the conventions of rhetoric; Jaques proves interested enough to ask for a recounting of the seven "degrees of the lie" (88-9).

At last, the undisguised Rosalind and Celia arrive, led by Hymen, the Greek god of marriage, who speaks in blank verse with three or four feet per line, as opposed to Shakespeare's usual iambic pentameter, which has five feet. After Duke Senior and Orlando rejoice in Rosalind's appearance, Hymen proceeds to wed each of the four couples: Orlando and Rosalind, Oliver and Celia, Silvius and Phebe, and Touchstone and Audrey. After a "wedlock hymn" (137), Jaques de Boys, the brother between Oliver and Orlando, arrives to announce news: Duke Frederick, having embarked on a military journey into the forest in search of the banished Duke Senior, was converted to goodness by "an old religious man" (160) and bequeathed the crown and all his land back to his brother. Duke Senior implores the company to fully enjoy the "rustic revelry" (177) before returning to courtly life. The philosophizing Jaques then bids farewell to the company, naming the good fortunes that all the men have happened upon, to join the converted Duke Frederick, from whom he expects "there is much matter to be heard and learned" (185). The play closes with dancing.

Epilogue

The character of Rosalind bids farewell to the audience with the hope that women and men alike found enjoyment in the play. Since in Shakespeare's time the actor playing Rosalind was a man, he notes that he would have even kissed some of the men in the audience had he been a woman; instead, he simply asks that they bid him farewell.

Characters

Adam

Adam is an aged servant of the de Boys household. Adam bolsters Orlando's claim to having the strongest ties to his father by calling Orlando a "memory / Of old sir Rowland" (2.3.3-4) and by accompanying him in exile, going so far as to offer his life's savings to ensure the young man's survival.

Aliena

See Celia

Amiens

Amiens is a courtier attending Duke Senior in exile.

Audrey

Audrey is a country wench who herds goats and who marries Touchstone. Audrey is portrayed as especially ignorant, not even understanding Touchstone's ridicule of her.

Celia

Celia is Duke Frederick's daughter and

Rosalind's cousin. Celia shares a powerful bond with Rosalind, voluntarily accompanying her cousin into exile after remarking, "Shall we be sund'red, shall we part, sweet girl? / No, let my father seek another heir" (96-7). While Rosalind is given far more attention, Celia serves as the catalyst for some of her cousin's thoughts and actions. After Orlando's victory, she states, "Gentle cousin, / Let us go thank him and encourage him" (1.2.229-30); when Rosalind is banished, even before she thinks to visit her father, Celia suggests first that they go "to seek my uncle in the forest of Arden" (1.3.105), then that they wear disguises. Celia poses as a peasant woman named Aliena.

Unlike Celia, her cousin Rosalind seems unable to assume the masculine role without disparaging the feminine. After Rosalind speaks of women's ways with Orlando, Celia scolds her for her remarks about women. Thus, Celia may be viewed as a stronger woman than her cousin.

Charles

Charles is Duke Frederick's wrestler, who fights Orlando in act 1, scene 2. Oliver tricks Charles into believing that Orlando is a villain and that Charles should thus do as much damage to Orlando as possible. However, despite this instruction, Charles is defeated by Orlando.

Corin

Corin is an old shepherd who befriends Rosalind, Celia, and Touchstone. While Touchstone abuses him for his simplicity, Corin is stalwart and genuine in his defense of his pastoral life: "I am a true laborer; I earn that I eat, get that I wear, owe no man hate, envy no man's happiness" (73-5).

Jaques de Boys

Jaques is the second son of Sir Rowland de Boys and is Oliver and Orlando's brother. The news of Duke Frederick's conversion is delivered by Jaques de Boys, who serves as a neutral mediator between the good and evil forces of the play.

Duke Frederick

Frederick is Duke Senior's younger brother and usurper of his throne. He is also Celia's father and Rosalind's uncle. Duke Frederick is a fairly one-dimensional villain through most of the play; his base nature is aptly summed up by Le Beau: "this Duke / Hath ta'en displeasure 'gainst his gentle niece, *Grounded upon no other argument* But that the people praise her for her virtues / And pity her for her good father's sake" (267-71). Reflecting his irrelevant status as a character, he does not even make an appearance after being converted by an "old religious man" (5.4.160) in the forest.

Duke Senior

The exiled elder brother of Duke Frederick and

father of Rosalind, Duke Senior serves as the benevolent patriarchal figure of the Forest of Arden. He utters the first lines in the forest as well as the rhyming couplet that closes the play. His introduction to the forest is essential in establishing the setting's superiority—"Are not these woods / More free from peril than the envious court?" (2.1.3-4)—while also addressing its drawbacks: "the icy fang *And churlish chiding of the winter's wind ... these are counselors* That feelingly persuade me what I am" (2.1.6-11). That is, Duke Senior fairly delights even in the physical sensation of being cold, which makes him feel far more alive than did the "painted pomp" (2.1.3) of the court.

Ganymede

See Rosalind

Hymen

The Greek god of marriage, Hymen appears in the final scene to marry all the couples. The personification of the god gives substance to the forest's otherworldliness.

Jaques

Jaques is a melancholy lord attending Duke Senior in banishment. Jaques is commonly considered Touchstone's foil, as he provides commentary on the play's diverse issues from a completely different perspective. Jaques's misanthropy, or distaste for humanity, initially casts a dark shadow over the events in Arden forest. Where Duke Senior expresses regret at the killing of the "native burghers of this desert city" (2.1.23)—the deer—"in their own confines" (2.1.24) essentially as an afterthought, Jaques weeps at the sight and sound of a wounded deer pouring forth tears and heaving its last breaths. As reported by a lord, Jaques goes so far as to "most invectively ... pierceth through *The body of the country, city, court,* Yea, and of this our life, swearing that we *Are mere usurpers, tyrants" (2.1.58-61). Thus, while Duke Senior has already been cast as a virtuous man, in contrast to the usurper Frederick, Jaques characterizes not only the elder duke but also all the men who have invaded the forest as usurpers in turn. The melancholy philosophizer can be seen as something of an environmentalist. Jaques's antihumanism is highlighted when Duke Senior's party is unable to locate him and one lord remarks, "I think he be transformed into a beast,* For I can nowhere find him like a man" (2.7.1-2).

Overall, the audience does not develop a favorable impression of Jaques. While Jaques reveals a certain fondness for Touchstone and professes his own desire to become a fool, so as to better "Cleanse the foul body of th' infected world" (2.7.60), Duke Senior promptly discredits him for having been a "libertine, / As sensual as the brutish sting itself" (2.7.65-6). Indeed, Jaques is something of a parody of an Elizabethan stereotype (and of a number of Shakespeare's contemporary satirists), the traveler who returns from abroad only to become discontented with domestic life. Shakespeare shows no sympathy for Jaques throughout the play: his cynical statements are rebuked time and again by Rosalind, Orlando, Touchstone, and Duke Senior. Even the initial portrayal of Jaques as an environmentalist is negated when he revels later in the killing of a second deer, hailing the successful hunter as a "Roman conqueror" (4.2.3-4); the text gives no evidence that the line would have been delivered ironically.

In the end, Jaques refuses to take part in the wedding celebration even vicariously, noting, "I am for other than for dancing measures" (5.4.193), and many commentators have read this as Shakespeare's ultimate condemnation of Jaques's character: he simply can not take part in life's joys. Yet while most of the protagonists will be returning to the oft-decried courtly life, Jaques intends to join the newly religious Duke Frederick, remarking, "Out of these convertites / There is much matter to be heard and learned" (5.4.184-85). His final lines, which are somewhat cryptic—"what you would have / I'll stay to know at your abandoned cave" (5.4.195-96)—at the very least indicate that he is devoted to the ideal of the pastoral world, rather than having merely vacationed there out of necessity.

Le Beau

One of Duke Frederick's courtiers, Le Beau serves as an intermediary between Duke Frederick and his daughter and niece, telling the two women of the wrestling match and also of the duke's ill humor after its conclusion.

Sir Oliver Mar-text

Sir Oliver is a vicar whose marriage of Touchstone and Audrey is interrupted by Jaques.

Oliver

Oliver is the eldest son of Sir Rowland de Boys. Oliver is expressly villainous, remarking that he dislikes Orlando largely because the latter is so virtuous and generally well loved by others. This animosity parallels that harbored by Duke Frederick toward the deceased Sir Rowland de Boys, highlighting the degree to which both men are antagonized by the "honorable" (1.2.215). At the end, Orlando's compassion for Oliver inspires the elder brother to bequeath Sir Rowland's estate to the younger; Oliver subsequently marries Celia.

Orlando

The youngest son of Sir Rowland de Boys, Orlando serves as the play's romantic male hero, eventually marrying Rosalind. Orlando's appearances in the first act well establish his moral virtue, as he craves only "such exercises as may become a gentleman" (1.1.69-70), including a good education, while Oliver, the eldest de Boys brother, professes to despise Orlando expressly because the younger is "so much in the heart of the world, and especially of my own people, who best know him, that I am altogether misprized" (1.1.161-63). Orlando proceeds to outwrestle Charles, a Goliath figure, without boast or bravado, and he even proves humbly shy when Rosalind addresses him afterward.

Much attention is given to Orlando's ties to his father, Rowland, whose name is a loose anagram of his youngest son's. Their last name, meanwhile, comes from *bois*, which means "forest" in French. When Orlando reiterates the claim, "The spirit of my father grows strong in me" (1.1.67-8), the audience understands that Orlando, not Oliver, is the true heir to the virtuous natural world signified by their last name.

In the Forest of Arden, the audience's impression of Orlando shifts somewhat, as Rosalind, posing as Ganymede, appears to control, if not dominate, the interactions between the destined pair. The audience may feel that Orlando's inability to direct their conversations reflects a lack of masculine assertiveness. Yet in fact, one of Orlando's surest virtues may be his ability to reconcile himself to more feminine qualities. Upon reaching the forest realm of Duke Senior, Orlando first adopts an aggressive stance; however, once he realizes he is being kindly received, he remarks, "Let gentleness my strong enforcement be; / In the which hope I blush, and hide my sword" (2.7.118-19). With Duke Senior serving as a surrogate father figure to Orlando, this scene might be viewed from a Freudian perspective as a resolution of the hostility toward the father associated with the Oedipus complex. Signaling that resolution, Orlando taps his nurturing side, noting, "like a doe, I go to find my fawn" (128). In "Sexual Politics and Social Structure," with reference to Orlando's later rescue of Oliver, Peter B. Erickson observes that the youngest brother "achieves a synthesis of attributes traditionally labeled masculine and feminine when he combines compassion and aggression in rescuing his brother from the lioness" (231).

Ultimately, as Erickson relates, Orlando is confirmed as the foremost authority figure in both his relationship with Rosalind and in the play as a whole. The possession of Rosalind in a literal sense passes from Duke Senior to Orlando. When Duke Senior is restored as the head of the dukedom, his possessions will pass not to his daughter but to the husband of his daughter, meaning that Orlando will inherit the entire land. Thus, as Erickson concludes, "Festive celebration is now possible because a dependable, that is, patriarchal, social order is securely in place" (232).

Phebe

Phebe is a shepherdess. She is indifferent toward Silvius, who is courting her, and falls in love with Ganymede instead. She eventually agrees to marry Silvius.

Rosalind

The exiled Duke Senior's daughter and niece of Duke Frederick, Rosalind is the play's central character, in that she has both the most lines and brings about much of the play's resolution. She is downhearted from the beginning, as her father has been away in exile, and only when her heart is "overthrown" (1.2.244) are her spirits first lifted. Leaving the court in banishment, along with her fleeing cousin, she adopts the disguise of a man, Ganymede, largely so that she and Celia may appear less vulnerable to any would-be assailants. At this point, she endeavors to transform herself outwardly and bear "a swashing and a martial outside" (1.3.118), that is, a swaggering, confrontational demeanor. Nevertheless, she confesses to yet also bearing "hidden woman's fear" (1.3.117), and many of her lines in the forest reflect her attempts to reconcile her maidenly reserve with her intent to pass as a man.

In posing as Ganymede, Rosalind draws upon her ample reserves of wit, which, as a courtly lady in Elizabethan times, she may not have had much opportunity to use otherwise. When she intends to treat Orlando like "a saucy lackey" (3.2.292), she guides the conversation with her witty remarks on the passage of time. She then arranges for Orlando to dote upon her, in her disguise as Ganymede, as if she were Rosalind, ensuring a sustained connection with him. She later lectures Orlando on the appearances and actions of one who is truly love struck.

Though liberated in terms of the attitude she

can adopt around Orlando, Rosalind otherwise professes to be constrained by her disguise. As she, Celia, and Touchstone enter the forest, she notes a desire to "disgrace my man's apparel, and to cry like a woman" (2.4.4-5). Similarly, when she faints at the news of Orlando's having suffered a grievous wound, she rises and first utters, "I would I were at home" (4.3.162), then reflexively negates her emotional state, claiming she had counterfeited the swoon. The audience is left to decide whether such denials are positive steps for a woman of that era to take.

Regardless of how much Rosalind revels in her man's disguise, the play's closure is very much a return to a state of female subservience. Indeed, from the outset, Rosalind is understood to be depressed largely because of the absence of any male figure in her life: her father has been exiled, and the fact that she only grows animated upon meeting Orlando sheds light upon her earlier suggestion that they divert themselves by "falling in love" (1.2.24). Before revealing her identity, Rosalind refers to herself in speaking to her father as "your Rosalind" (5.4.6) and requests confirmation that he will "bestow her on Orlando" (5.4.7). Regarding Rosalind's return to her womanhood, Peter B. Erickson notes, "A benevolent patriarchy still requires women to be subordinate, and Rosalind's final performance is her enactment of this subordination" (232). Erickson also notes that the epilogue, in which the male actor playing Rosalind reveals himself as male, presents a "further phasing out of Rosalind" (233).

Silvius

Silvius is a shepherd who remains in love with the shepherdess Phebe despite her constant scorning. He eventually marries her.

Touchstone

A fool in the service of first Oliver, then Rosalind and Celia, Touchstone is all that his name implies: he acts as a touchstone, testing the qualities of the other characters both at Duke Frederick's court and in the forest. He also is an apt persona for conveying bits and piece of philosophy to the audience, whether they be genuine or ironic. Many commentators have noted that Touchstone differs from the fools in Shakespeare's preceding plays largely because the playwright shaped the part to a different actor: Robert Armin. Armin, who himself wrote a work on the varying natures of court fools, was perhaps fit to play a jester of greater sophistication than the man he replaced within the Lord Chamberlain's Men, Will Kempe, who had proven successful playing strictly comic roles. In fact, Armin may have joined the company midway through Shakespeare's writing of *As You Like It*, which would account for the difference in Touchstone's temperament in the first act as compared to the later acts; in "Touchstone in Arcadia," Robert H. Goldsmith notes that this change may also simply reflect the respective degrees of intellectual freedom that Touchstone felt at court and in the forest, as any court fool would have been wise to restrain his wit somewhat in the presence of a usurper.

Touchstone is perhaps more out of place in the Forest of Arden than any other character in the play. While Touchstone marries Audrey at the end, the audience understands that he does so merely to enjoy the associated conjugal rights. Otherwise, throughout much of the play Touchstone remarks not on the merrier aspects of the forest but on what the forest lacks as compared to the court, as in his remarks to Corin about the shepherd's life, where he expresses the negative view: "in respect that it is a shepherd's life, it is naught ... in respect that it is private, it is a very vile life ... in respect it is not in the court, it is tedious ... as there is no more plenty in it, it goes much against my stomach" (3.2.14-21).

In general, Touchstone looks at every situation from an oblique angle and speaks in a caustic voice. He sees Orlando's poetry not as charming but pedantic; he insists that Corin is a sinner for having never learned court manners; and rather than enjoying their song, he condemns the pages as being off time. He even refuses to acknowledge himself as either witty or a fool: to Rosalind he states, "I shall ne'er be ware of mine own wit till I break my shins against it" (2.4.56-7), while Jaques recalls him remarking, "Call me not fool till heaven hath sent me fortune" (2.7.19). Goldsmith sums up Touchstone's role in part by quoting C. S. Lewis, who notes in *The Allegory of Love* that a tale in the mode of *As You Like It* "protects itself against the laughter of the vulgar ... by allowing laughter and cynicism their place *inside* the poem" (199). Goldsmith himself notes, "Touchstone's presence within the pastoral romance is a concession to our sense of comic realism and protects the play from corrosive criticism" (200). Indeed, Touchstone's sarcastic rejoinders quite likely preempted just such unruly commentary from the groundlings at the Globe Theatre.

William

William is a country fellow who loves Audrey and is rudely threatened by Touchstone.

Themes

Pastoral Life

Numerous oppositions in *As You Like It* reveal Shakespeare's partiality toward the pastoral rustic life of Arden forest to life at court. At Duke Frederick's court, disorder holds sway. The deterioration of political authority is the most obvious form of disorder, for Duke Frederick has unlawfully seized Duke Senior's kingdom. This political degeneration is compounded by a more personal disorder, since the dukes are also brothers at odds with each other. This conflict is also underscored by the antagonistic relationship of two other brothers at the court, Oliver and Orlando. Arden forest offers a sense of pure, spiritual order in contrast to the corrupt condition of Duke Frederick's court. Indeed, Duke Senior, who introduces the audience to the forest, immediately establishes the realm as a haven from the court, which he refers to as a place of "painted pomp" and as "envious"—that is, a place where people covet what others have—in opposition to the virtual absence of both private property and social position in the wild.

Meanwhile, for those fleeing the court, the journey to the forest is long and difficult; when the characters arrive they are physically exhausted and hungry. The harsh experience of returning to nature acts as a stripping process, however, laying bare the characters' virtuous natures calloused by court life. Some characters, like Orlando and Rosalind, need little improvement and find in Arden a liberation from the oppression they have endured at court. Others, such as Oliver and Duke Frederick, approach the forest with malicious intent only to undergo a complete spiritual reformation. Arden is thus a morally pure realm whose special curative powers purge and renew the forest dwellers, granting them a self-awareness that they will ultimately use to restore order at court.

Fortune vs. Nature

Closely allied with the opposition of court life and the Forest of Arden is the dichotomy between fortune and nature. Here, "fortune" represents both material gain—achieved through power, birthright, or possessions—and a force that unpredictably determines events. "Nature," on the other hand, is both the purifying force of Arden and humanity's fundamental condition stripped of the trappings of wealth, power, and material possessions.

The opposition between fortune and nature is highlighted most in the first act, where the audience finds that fortune has benefited the villainous (Frederick and Oliver) over the virtuous (Duke Senior, Orlando, and Rosalind). Celia suggests that she and Rosalind "mock the good housewife Fortune from her wheel, that her gifts may henceforth be bestowed equally" (1.2.30-2), referring to the fact that the goddess Fortune was historically depicted as blind, sitting on a spherical throne, with one foot on a ball and one hand upon her wheel that determined the fates of everyone. The goddess Nature, meanwhile, was considered to be in control of people's innate virtues, such as their nobility and wisdom. In this scene, Rosalind and Celia discuss Fortune and Nature at length, musing on the two goddesses' effects on the world.

Duke Senior is presented as a man who has successfully thwarted Fortune; after his speech praising the rustic over the courtly life, Amiens notes, "Happy is your Grace *That can translate the stubbornness of fortune* Into so quiet and so sweet a style" (18-20). Fortune is mentioned again later by Adam, who, upon fleeing with Orlando, notes, in a rhyming couplet closing a scene, "Yet fortune cannot recompense me better *Than to die well and not my master's debtor" (2.4.75-6). Nature, meanwhile, is invoked most pointedly when Oliver describes his brother's rescue of him: "But kindness, nobler ever than revenge* And nature, stronger than his just occasion, *Made him give battle to the lioness,* Who quickly fell before him" (4.3.129-32). Thus, the play's protagonists by and large manage to overcome the caprices of Fortune by drawing on the assets of Nature.

Time

Time is also contrasted in the court scenes and in the Forest of Arden. At court, time is referred to in specific terms, marked by definite intervals, in most cases in relation to the duke's threats: he orders Rosalind to leave the court within ten days or she will be executed, and he gives Oliver one year to find Orlando or else his land and possessions will be confiscated. In Arden, however, the meaning of time is less precise. In his first meeting with Jaques, Touchstone provides a slightly whimsical rumination on time; he seems to be remarking on his sense that he is simply rotting away in the uneventful forest. Jaques later offers a disheartened perception of how time passes predictably for all men, as his "Seven Ages of Man" speech illustrates the individual's passage through life in predetermined stages, ending with the image of man as a pathetically ineffectual and dependent creature.

When Rosalind, posing as Ganymede, first addresses Orlando, she asks him, "what is 't o'clock?" (3.2.296), and his response is especially meaningful: "You should ask me, what time o' day. There's no clock in the forest" (3.2.297-98). Indeed, time in Arden is measured "in divers paces with divers persons" (3.2.304-05), as Rosalind subsequently instructs Orlando; the lover's constant sighing and groaning, she contends, ought to be as regular as clockwork, while a young maid, a priest, and a thief would all feel time's passage uniquely. Later on, Rosalind lectures Orlando for not being more punctual, because a true lover would not lose a single moment that he could be spending with his beloved. In general, the sense that time is a subjective, not an objective, quality enhances Arden's mythical and romantic aspects.

Sexual Identity

Sexual identity is examined primarily through the character of Rosalind, who disguises herself as a man named Ganymede—a mythological boy whose name was synonymous with beauty and androgyny—to ensure her safe passage to Arden. Though she can discard her male costume when she reaches the forest, Rosalind does not do so until the end of the play. Critics generally agree that she continues to act as Ganymede because the disguise liberates her from the submissive role of a woman. As a man, she is able to take more control of her own life, especially in her courtship with Orlando. In their playacting scenes, Rosalind controls the tactics of courtship in a way that is usually reserved for men, inverting their roles to teach Orlando the meaning of real love rather than love based on his idealized vision of her. An added complexity of Rosalind's sexual identity is evident if we consider that in Shakespeare's age, boys played the roles of women in dramas. The playwright takes advantage of this convention in *As You Like It* to accentuate flexibility in the presentation of gender. As the boy actor who performs as Rosalind must also play Ganymede, who in turn pretends to be Rosalind in the playacting sessions with Orlando, the audience follows the character's various transformations and can better appreciate the extent to which Rosalind's presentation of herself as masculine or feminine changes the way the other characters interact with her.

Acting and the Stage

References to acting, role-playing, scenes, and the stage are scattered throughout *As You Like It*, most prominently in reference to Rosalind's posing as Ganymede. When first meeting Orlando in the forest, she aims to "play the knave with him" (3.2.293); aside from her own role as a self-confident man, which is overlaid with her role as the fickle "Rosalind," she has much to say to Orlando about his playing the role of the lover, noting that he lacks the proper disheveled attire and that he is not as punctual as a lover ought to be. At one point she even entreats Celia to conduct a pretend marriage ceremony between herself and Orlando.

Such references to acting would be natural, of course, in the context of a play presented on the spare stage of the Globe Theatre, where boys and men played the parts of the women and, generally speaking, the artifice of the production could not be ignored. However, the passage in which Jaques delivers the "Seven Ages of Man" speech accentuates the theatrical aspect beyond what is found in Shakespeare's other works. After the arrival of Orlando, who tells of the exhausted Adam, Duke Senior observes, "This wide and universal theater *Presents more woeful pageants than the scene* Wherein we play in" (2.7.137-39). With these remarks, referring to both tragedy and drama, the duke lends gravity to Jaques's ensuing speech, about which Shakespearean commentators disagree. Some consider that Adam's consequent arrival is a negation of Jaques's speech as serious philosophy, in that the elderly man has just completed a substantial journey; on the other hand, Adam only reaches the realm of the duke because he has been carried by Orlando—as if he is indeed in the throes of the "second childishness" (2.7.165) Jaques has just described.

The central theme of Jaques's speech, that a single man goes through seven stages, or acts, in the course of his lifetime, echoes similar life-stage theories put forth by ancient thinkers, and the opening line, "All the world's a stage" (2.7.139), was said to adorn the Globe Theatre itself. The speech is rich in detail and imagery, as Jaques paints miniature portraits of each of the stages of man's life, and as fits his character, he highlights the ridiculous, helpless, or ineffectual aspects of each stage. The baby is "mewling and puking" (144), while the schoolboy whines as he is forced to attend school against his will. The lover's sentiments are made to seem absurd and extreme, as he sadly sings of "his mistress' eyebrow" (149), of all possible body parts. The soldier seems to live in isolation from society and friendship, "full of strange oaths" (150), as if belonging to a secret guild, and he is guided by negative, aggressive emotions like jealousy and anger; even when faced with the prospect of death, "in the cannon's mouth" (153), he still gives priority to his reputation. The justice's belly is understood to be lined with capon—a castrated rooster, which serves as another symbol of the impotence of living creatures—because judges were often bribed with capons. As a judge, meanwhile, both his physical appearance and his intellectual state—he is "full of wise saws and modern instances" (156), that is, he does not truly think independently—show him to be fulfilling his function in society without much thought or ability. Jaques's closing descriptions of the pantaloon and of the senile old man offer a vivid picture of every man's descent into obscurity: the pantaloon finds his body and his voice alike shrinking, while the final stage "is second childishness and mere oblivion" (165). Thus, in Jaques's view, not only does man pass through a number of predictable stages but also within each stage the depth of his person is no greater than that of a stock character in a play, meriting a psychological description of a few lines at most. Regardless of how Shakespeare meant the "Seven Ages of Man" speech to be interpreted, its insistence that all men are simply following the scripts of their lives—as cowritten by Fortune and Nature—is thought provoking.

Topics for Further Study

- In posing as Ganymede, Rosalind takes advantage of her disguise to comfortably interact with Orlando as if she were another man. Imagine the two roles reversed: Orlando has disguised himself as a woman in order to interact more comfortably with Rosalind. Conduct research on Elizabethan gender roles, and write an essay describing the ways in which such a role reversal would differ from the original situation. Then write a short prose piece portraying a meeting between Rosalind and the disguised Orlando.

- Read Thomas Lodge's *Rosalynde* (the source for Shakespeare's *As You Like It*). Write an essay comparing and contrasting the characters of Rosalynde, from Lodge's work, and Rosalind, from Shakespeare's. Also, why do you think Shakespeare altered the character the way he did?

- Research the way religions have affected patterns of marriage in different parts of the world. Relate your findings to the class, making reference to at least two non-Western cultures.

- Time is one of the major themes of *As You Like It*. Write an essay on how you have felt the passage of time at different points in your own life, making reference to various passages in the play that relate to or contrast with your personal experience.

- Shakespeare devotes much attention to the roles of the goddesses Fortune and Nature in Elizabethan life, specifically in the lives of his characters. Write an essay describing how modern life has been shaped by Fortune and Nature, making reference to passages describing the two forces in *As You Like It*, and explaining how the balance between them has shifted over time.

The references to acting, roles, and theater in *As You Like It* may best be interpreted in the context of the play as contrasted with the pastoral life. The characters of *As You Like It*, coming from the upper echelons of the court, would have been accustomed to civilization's comforts; while speaking with Corin, Touchstone regrets the absence of certain aspects of that courtly life, namely the abundances of society and food. Other characters function better than Touchstone in the forest milieu in that they are more willing or more able to "play the roles" of forest dwellers. In making frequent reference to the conventions of dramaturgy, Shakespeare assists his urban crowds to lose themselves in the ethereal theater of the Forest of Arden.

Style

The Pastoral

Traditionally, a pastoral is a poem focusing on shepherds and rustic life; it first appeared as a literary form in the third century C.E. The term itself is derived from *pastor*, the Latin word for "shepherd." A pastoral may contain artificial or unnatural elements, such as shepherd characters speaking with courtly eloquence or appearing in aristocratic dress. This poetic convention evolved over centuries until many of its features were incorporated into prose and drama. It was in these literary forms that pastoralism influenced English literature from about 1550 to 1750, most often as pastoral romance, a model featuring songs and characters with traditional pastoral aspects. Many of these elements can be seen in the source for Shakespeare's play, Thomas Lodge's popular pastoral novel *Rosalynde*, written in 1590. But by the time Shakespeare adapted Lodge's tale into *As You Like It* nearly a decade later, many pastoral themes were considered trite.

As a result, Shakespeare treated pastoralism ambiguously in the comedy. Without doubt, the audience is meant to be intoxicated by the carefree atmosphere of the forest along with the main characters, who are essentially given the freedom to concern themselves only with romantic love. The image of Orlando dashing from tree to tree hanging up his poems is perhaps the most emblematic of the play as a whole. Also, with the usurper Frederick as the head of the dukedom and the magnanimous Duke Senior overseeing life in the forest, each setting is endowed with the characteristics of its figurehead; the connotations of the forest are almost exclusively positive. In the speech in which Duke Senior introduces Arden, he praises the "tongues in trees, books in the running brooks, / Sermons in stones, and good in everything" (2.1.16-7).

On the other hand, the audience is rarely given respite from Jaques, whose melancholy is not really lessened by the forest, and Touchstone, who incessantly disparages both forest life in Arden and forest dwellers. While some of Touchstone's comments are merely absurd—such as portraying Corin as a sinner for not having been at court—their presence nonetheless prevents a wholly idealistic tone from taking over. Perhaps most tellingly, the comedy's resolution entails the entire company returning to court rather than remaining in the forest. Overall, *As You Like It* can be viewed as either an endorsement or a satire of the literary form of the pastoral—and that duality is nowhere more evident than in the play's title. Take your choice.

Lyrical Interludes

Shakespeare emphasized the romantic, pastoral aspect of *As You Like It* by including a significant number of songs and poems. In all, five different songs are performed, more than in any other comedy, while the audience hears three poems read aloud, two of Orlando's—one of which is then parodied by Touchstone—and one of Phebe's. In addition, Touchstone offers a few pithy lines upon leaving Sir Oliver Mar-Text, and Hymen's lines, which are written in rhyming trimeter instead of Shakespeare's conventional pentameter, have an immediate poetic ring to them. All of these forms of verse are presented in the Forest of Arden, rather than in the court. Meanwhile, more than half of the play is written in prose, aptly contrasting the characters' offhand everyday discourse with their romantic poetic bursts.

The texts of these songs are generally relevant to the scene in which they appear or to the play as a whole. The fifth scene of the second act seems to exist exclusively as a framework for the first tune, sung by Amiens, which mentions "the greenwood tree" (2.5.1), "the sweet bird's throat" (2.5.4), and "winter and rough weather" (2.5.7) and helps establish the woodland setting; Jaques's subsequent partly nonsensical verse, on the other hand, helps establish his nonconformity. The hunters' effusively masculine song, with its possibly sexual reference to "the horn, the horn, the lusty horn" (4.2.18), also essentially merits its own scene, highlighting the camaraderie and sense of self-determination fostered by hunting for food together.

The song sung by Amiens when Duke Senior welcomes Orlando and Adam, "Blow, blow, thou winter wind" (2.7.174-90), merits particular attention. In each verse, Amiens first invokes the severity of nature in wintertime, then offers as a contrast the greater severity of men toward one another. The winter wind is harsh, but it is "not so unkind / As man's ingratitude" (175-76); the breath of that wind is "rude" (179), but at least it fails to bite, as does the tooth of man. The chorus affirms this trust in nature and mistrust of man, glorifying the "green holly" (180) before stating, "Most friendship is faining"—that is, perhaps, both *yearning* and *pretending* ("feigning")—"most loving mere folly" (181). In the second verse, although the freezing sky stings and warps waters, it is preferred to "benefits forgot" (186) and a "friend rememb'red not" (189). Especially given its location in the play as a whole—at the point when the sorrows of courtly life are being discarded, as food and shelter within the forest have been secured—this song may be interpreted as emblematic of the play as a whole, with its depiction of nature's rhythms, even when bitter, as preferable to the strife of men.

Marginalization of Plot

The plot of *As You Like It* is perhaps the least important plot in all of Shakespeare's plays, at least in terms of the consequences of problematic situations and people's actions. Indeed, the most negative critical comments have come from scholars who perceive carelessness or even indifference in Shakespeare's fabrication of the plot. Albert Gilman sums up this dearth in his introduction to the play:

> What is unusual is the extraordinary dispatch with which the plot unfolds. Almost everything that is to happen, happens in the first act.... In the ensuing acts Shakespeare scarcely concerns himself with the troubles that were introduced in the first act. Except for three short scenes we are always in Arden, where the dangers we are chiefly aware of are falling in love or being worsted in a discussion.

To close out the play, the two villains are abruptly converted from villainy, and the four couples are very speedily wed—Oliver and Celia before the audience has witnessed one private conversation between them.

At certain points, Shakespeare's offhand treatment of the plot almost escapes attention. When Rosalind, disguised as Ganymede, first chances across Orlando in Arden, she says, "I will speak to him like a saucy lackey, and under that habit play the knave with him. Do you hear, forester?" (3.2.292-94). As the scene moves along, the audience may not even have time to wonder why Rosalind fails to discard her disguise, though nothing is truly preventing her from doing so. Later, when she tries to persuade Orlando to accompany her and be cured of his lovesickness, after expressing mild skepticism that she can do so, he reverses himself and says, "Now, by the faith of my love, I will" (3.2.418). Thus, despite all her previous questioning about the sincerity of Orlando's love, Rosalind seems to ignore the fact that he follows her for the express purpose of falling out of love with her; if Orlando follows not to fall out of love but because he has already seen through her disguise, the audience is given no indication of that.

Shakespeare's summary treatment of the play's action seems above all to reflect that Shakespeare did not intend the plot of the play to be the essence of the play. In effect, limiting plot development allows for the greater development of the characters through casual, unforced, and thus particularly revealing, dialogue. Gilman, in highlighting the primacy of the dialogue and the characters' relationships in his introduction, playfully asks, "Who has not looked at his watch during the last act of a well-made plot and sighed to think of the knots still to be untied? We had rather be in Arden where the wicked are converted by fiat and lovers marry in half-dozen lots."

Similes

With the setting and atmosphere emphasized over the plot of *As You Like It*, the play depends heavily on imagery, as well as on wordplay introducing that imagery. In her essay "Image Establishes Atmosphere and Background in the Comedies," Caroline F. E. Spurgeon notes that certain types of comparisons are especially prevalent. Topical similes are those referring to scenes or objects that would have been familiar to the London-based Elizabethan audience. Rosalind's declaration to Orlando that she would "weep for nothing, like Diana in the fountain" (4.1.146-47) may be a reference to a fountain in the Cheapside district featuring a depiction of that goddess. Other topical similes in the text refer to the types of painted canvases that were hung on walls, the whipping treatment that madmen received, and the work of tavern employees. Sturgeon notes that the prominence of such references reflects the fact that Shakespeare was writing for "a highly sophisticated town audience, which delights in bouts of sparkling wit,... is ever alive to double meanings, and is quick as lightning to seize on and laugh at a local or topical allusion."

Similes mentioning animals are also found frequently in the text, more than in any other Shakespearean comedy, further emphasizing the natural world. Orlando compares himself to a doe seeking her fawn; Jaques likens himself to a weasel and to a rooster; and Rosalind compares herself to a cock-pigeon. Fittingly, the character who seems to be most in touch with his animal instincts invokes the images of a number of creatures in explaining to Jaques his intent to marry: "As the ox hath his bow, sir, the horse his curb, and the falcon her bells, so man hath his desires; and as pigeons bill, so wedlock would be nibbling" (3.3.76-9). Other natural objects and forces are likewise often brought to the spectators' attention. Orlando presents the image of a rotten tree; Touchstone that of fruit ripening and rotting; and Jaques that of rank weeds.

Mention of the weather, too, serves to enhance the sense of being outdoors, such as when Hymen utters to Touchstone and Audrey, "You and you are sure together / As the winter to foul weather" (5.4.135-36).

Historical Context

Gender Roles

The way Shakespeare addresses gender roles in *As You Like It* reflects the widespread sexism of the Elizabethan era, and thus the topic merits discussion not only in the fictional but also in the historical context. In his *Bedford Companion to Shakespeare*, Russ McDonald offers an assessment of the state of gender relations:

> That women occupied a position subordinate to men in the early modern period is beyond dispute; that this was the 'natural' state of affairs was almost beyond dispute. Although the idea is repugnant to modern sensibilities, most thinkers in the sixteenth century took it as axiomatic that men are superior to women.

Indeed, many gendered notions are presented not simply through the opinions of certain characters but as established facts, illustrating for the modern reader the common beliefs of the era. In the course of the discussion on the goddesses Fortune and Nature, Rosalind states, "the bountiful blind woman doth most mistake in her gifts to women" (1.2.34-5), and Celia agrees, noting that "those that she makes fair, she scarce makes honest, and those that she makes honest, she makes very ill-favoredly" (1.2.36-8). That is, the story's leading women evidently see beauty and chastity, which are deemed typically exclusive, as the only female qualities worth discussing. Other characteristics attributed to women, as reflected in the play's dialogue, include "fear" (1.3.117), which Rosalind hopes to hide under man's apparel, and excessive emotionality; Rosalind feels obliged to suppress her tears when she, Celia, and Touchstone enter the forest in utter exhaustion, and when she faints at the news of Orlando's wound, Oliver exclaims, "You a man! You lack a man's heart" (4.3.164-65).

Rosalind and Celia refer to the marketability of women—not merely objectifying themselves but even suggesting that they have a quantifiable value—twice later on: Celia notes that if they learn news from Le Beau they will be "the more marketable" (1.2.93), while Rosalind, as Ganymede, tells Phebe, "Sell when you can, you are not for all markets" (3.5.60). This most likely reflects the fact that a potential bride customarily offered a dowry to her suitor, consisting of whatever capital and property her family could afford. The existence of the dowry is also important to consider with respect to the romantic context of the play. McDonald notes,

> Marriage was part of a system of inheritance and economics so ingrained and pervasive that the emotional affectations or physical desires of a man and woman diminished in importance. This was

> especially true among the upper classes ... where marriage was regarded as a convenient instrument for joining or ensuring peace between two powerful families, for consolidating land holdings, or for achieving other familial, financial, or even political ends.

Thus the Forest of Arden is an idealized pastoral setting not only in the immediacy of nature and the absence of the trappings of courtly life but also in the fact that the play's strictly romantic liaisons, especially between Rosalind and Orlando, might have been impossible in the context of the court.

While women of the time were certainly constrained by male perceptions of their femininity, men were perhaps similarly constrained by perceptions of their masculinity. Phebe finds herself falling not for the beseeching, pitiable Silvius but for the coarse, aggressive Ganymede. She states, "'Tis but a peevish boy; yet he talks well" (3.5.110), then adds, "But sure he's proud. And yet his pride becomes him. / He'll make a proper man" (3.5.115). Later, in turn, in that Phebe's letter has "a boisterous and a cruel style" (4.3.32), Rosalind assumes that it must have been "a man's invention, and his hand" (4.3.30). Ultimately, however, Shakespeare may have played a significant role in softening the perception of the masculine, if not in hardening the perception of the feminine; Peter B. Erickson offers some enlightening commentary on gender relations of the Elizabethan era as modified by the theater: "The convention of males playing female roles gives men the opportunity to imagine sex-role fluidity and flexibility. Built into the conditions of performance is the potential for male acknowledgment of a 'feminine self' and thus for male transcendence of a narrow masculinity." In that they did not themselves appear on the stage, women were not truly given the same opportunity to test the boundaries of their gender roles.

Rural Life

While the term *urban* would not be coined until 1619, at the beginning of the seventeenth century London was without doubt an essentially urban locale, with a total population of some two hundred thousand. Thus life in the city would have been remarkably different from life in the countryside, with the residents of the respective milieus perhaps perceiving one another as virtual foreigners. Shakespeare drew on these differences heavily in *As You Like It*, juxtaposing aristocrats and philosophers from the upper echelons of the dukedom like Jaques and Touchstone with simplistic woodland folk like William and Audrey. The conversations between the educated and the uneducated are some of the most comical of the play. Overall, the importance of the setting may have been relatively small, as the stage would not have been decorated with any backdrop or props conjuring the feel of the forest; only the actors' words and costumes and the spectators' imaginations would have placed the action in the fictional forest. Further, Shakespeare focuses foremost on the love stories, not on the practicalities of forest life.

The English Satirists

The character of Jaques has been recognized not only as a fairly common Elizabethan literary personage—the traveler who has returned home to be generally discontented with life—but also as a representative of a group of satirists writing during Shakespeare's lifetime. Englishmen who had availed themselves of the satiric format to address the era's social conditions included John Davies, John Harington, Ben Jonson, Thomas Bastard, and John Weaver. An order put forth by the monarchy on June 1, 1599, called for the burning of many satirical works and banned any future production of work of that genre. Shakespearean scholars have assumed that when Celia states, "Since the little wit that fools have was silenced, the little foolery that wise men have makes a great show" (1.2.85-7), the line is meant to refer to the 1599 order.

Compare & Contrast

- **Elizabethan era:** Marriages are often conducted not for the sake of love but for the sake of money, property, or even reputation. Especially among the upper classes, brides brought substantial dowries to their husbands, and the consolidation of wealth between two families could shape political alliances. By law, firstborn sons always inherited the estate of the father, where in families with no sons, the firstborn daughter inherited the estate—to be passed on to her future husband.

Modern era: Marriages among most people in most Western countries are conducted for the sake of the romantic interests of the two parties. Personal wills, rather than estate laws, govern the passing of property and capital from the deceased to their descendants, such that a marriage is no guarantee of earning a substantial inheritance. Still, people occasionally marry more for the sake of money than for the sake of love; some notorious modern cases include those in which the very young have married the very old, if not the dying.

- **Elizabethan era:** With portable clocks still large enough to be cumbersome and only accurate to the nearest fifteen minutes, the passage of time cannot be conceived of definitely. People would not carry timepieces on their person—except sundials, such as the one Touchstone pulls from his pocket while speaking with Jaques. A forested area would truly have no clocks about; people familiar with courtly life might have appreciated that absence of timepieces.

Modern era: Clocks are constructed in all shapes and sizes, analog and digital, and are everywhere. Virtually all activities conducted within the confines of greater civilization revolve around the precise passage of time. In the age of cell phones, digital signals ensure that the time shown on displays is exactly correct. Many people, especially those involved in the business world, carry watches to ensure their awareness of the hour and their ability to arrive at certain places at certain times. Perhaps especially in the wilderness, most people are careful to bring timepieces so as to know the nearness of sunset and not be caught in the dark.

- **Elizabethan era:** In 1599, by royal order some satires were removed from circulation and the future publication of satires was banned outright. Consequently, the demolition of London playhouses was ordered.

Modern era: While laws against libel and slander prevent fabricated and hurtful accusations against any individuals, honest and biting commentaries are allowed in almost all forms of media. However, in certain media the content conveyed to audiences is regulated outside the legal system by entities other than governmental ones; for example, television programs are largely sponsored by advertisers and if advertising dollars cannot be raised, programs cannot be broadcast, meaning that corporate commercial interests often control the kinds of information and images available to television viewers. In media realms where the audiences pay the bulk of revenues, content is usually tailored to a target audience. The advent of the Internet and the widespread production of personal Web sites has both increased and distilled the dissemination of ideas and information.

One characteristic of the English satirists was that they restricted their commentary to impersonal, generic claims, such that they could not be accused of targeting any individuals in particular. In expressing his desire to become a fool so as to safely comment on society's ills, Jaques notes that he would not "tax any private party" (2.7.71) but would speak broadly and allow anyone who has done wrong to suit "his folly to the mettle of my speech" (2.7.82). In his text *Shakespeare's Satire*, Oscar James Campbell offers a succinct description of what the author may have intended to communicate to his audiences through his depiction of Jaques: "Shakespeare's ridicule of Jaques ... is amused disapproval of the headlong moral ardor which the satirists in both poem and play felt or pretended to feel. Such a temper, Shakespeare says, is ridiculous and utterly destructive to the comic spirit."

Critical Overview

Critical commentary on *As You Like It* over the centuries has tended to focus on two facts: first, that the plot itself is thin and treated perhaps with excessive haste by its author, and, second, that the essence of the play—ruminations on love, time, and nature—is certainly best conveyed in the context of a play that treats the plot in just such an offhand fashion. Different critics, then, have weighed the importance of these two factors differently.

As quoted in *The Complete Illustrated Shakespeare*, edited by Howard Staunton, the German scholar August von Schlegel perceived the play quite positively, summarily remarking:

> Throughout the whole picture, it seems to be the poet's design to show that to call forth the poetry which has its indwelling in nature and the human mind, nothing is wanted but to throw off all artificial constraint, and restore both to mind and nature their original liberty. In the very progress of the piece, the dreamy carelessness of such an existence is sensibly expressed: it is even alluded to by Shakespeare in the title.

As quoted in the same volume, the English scholar Nathan Drake notes, "Though this play, with the exception of the disguise and self-discovery of Rosalind, may be said to be destitute of plot, it is yet one of the most delightful of the dramas of Shakespeare." He goes on to observe: From the forest of Arden, from that wild wood of oaks,... from the bosom of sequestered glens and pathless solitudes, has the poet called forth lessons of the most touching and consolatory wisdom.... The effect of such scenery, on the lover of nature, is to take full possession of the soul, to absorb its very faculties, and, through the charmed imagination, to convert the workings of the mind into the sweetest sensations of the heart, into the joy of grief, into a thankful endurance of adversity, into the interchange of the tenderest affections.

In his introduction to the play, Albert Gilman notes, "Some critics have complained of inconsistencies in the plotting," as the length of time for which Duke Senior has been banished and the respective heights of Rosalind and Celia are referred to differently in different passages. Also, Shakespeare has perhaps for no good reason given the name of Jaques to both the melancholy philosopher and the brother of Oliver and Orlando. Regarding this fact, Helen Gardner notes: It seems possible that the melancholy Jaques began as this middle son and that his melancholy was in origin a scholar's melancholy. If so, the character changed as it developed, and by the time that Shakespeare had fully conceived his cynical spectator he must have realized that he could not be kin to Oliver and Orlando. The born solitary must have no family: Jaques seems the quintessential only child.

Gilman adds, "These bits of carelessness, if that is what they are, are not unusual in Shakespeare and not peculiar to this play." Gilman does note that another cause for critical concern is the lack of psychological complexity: "The motives of the chief characters in *As You Like It* are as simple and abrupt as the action of the play, and they could surely be put in evidence by those who think the play a piece of indifferent craftsmanship."

A somewhat comically negative take on the work can be found in George Bernard Shaw's play entitled *The Dark Lady of the Sonnets*. Gilman quotes a scene in which the character of Will Shakespeare remarks to Queen Elizabeth:

> I have also stole from a book of idle wanton tales two of the most damnable foolishness in the world, in the one of which a woman goeth in man's attire and maketh impudent love to her swain, who pleaseth the groundlings by overthrowing a wrestler.... I have writ these to save my friends from penury, yet shewing my scorn for such follies and for them that praise them by calling the one As You Like It, meaning that it is not as *I* like it.

Helen Gardner sums up the appeal of *As You Like It* by calling it "a play to please all tastes." After citing the simple asset of the romantic aspect of the tale, she observes:

For the learned and literary this is one of Shakespeare's most allusive plays, uniting old traditions and playing with them lightly.... *As You Like It* is the most refined and exquisite of the comedies, the one which is most consistently played over by a delighted intelligence. It is Shakespeare's most Mozartian comedy.

Sources

Brown, John Russell, "'As You Like It,'" in *Shakespeare's Dramatic Style*, Barnes & Noble, 1971, pp. 72-103.

Burgess, Anthony, *Shakespeare*, Knopf, 1970.

Campbell, Oscar James, "*As You Like It*," in *Shakespeare's Satire*, Oxford University Press, 1943.

Craig, Hardin, "*As You Like It*," in *An Interpretation of Shakespeare*, Citadel Press, 1949, pp. 122-24.

Erickson, Peter B., "Sexual Politics and Social Structure in *As You Like It*," by William Shakespeare, edited by Albert Gilman, New American Library, 1986, pp. 222-37.

Fergusson, Francis, "*As You Like It*," in *Shakespeare: The Pattern in His Carpet*, Delacorte Press, 1958, pp. 148-55.

Fink, Z. S., "Jaques and the Malcontent Traveler," in *Philological Quarterly*, Vol. 14, No. 2, April 1935, 237-52.

Gardner, Helen, "'As You Like It,'" in *As You Like It*, by William Shakespeare, New American Library, 1986, pp. 203-21.

Gilman, Albert, "Introduction," in *As You Like It*, by William Shakespeare, New American Library, 1986, pp. xx-xxxiii.

Goldsmith, Robert H., "Shakespeare's Wise Fools," in *Wise Fools in Shakespeare*, Michigan State University Press, 1955, pp. 47-67.

——————, "Touchstone in Arcadia," in *As You Like It*, by William Shakespeare, edited by Albert Gilman, New American Library, 1986, pp. 195-202.

Grice, Maureen, "*As You Like It*," in *The Reader's Encyclopedia of Shakespeare*, edited by Oscar James Campbell and Edward G. Quinn, Crowell, 1966, pp. 41-8.

Hunter, G. K. "*As You Like It*," in *The Later Comedies: "A Midsummer Night's Dream," "Much Ado About Nothing," "As You Like It," "Twelfth Night"*, British Council, 1962, pp. 32-43.

Jenkins, Harold, "*As You Like It*," in *Shakespeare Survey*, Vol. 7, 1955, pp. 40-51.

McDonald, Russ, *The Bedford Companion to Shakespeare*, 2nd ed., Bedford/St. Martin's, 2001.

Palmer, D. J., "*As You Like It* and the Idea of Play," in *Critical Quarterly*, Vol. 13, No. 3, Autumn 1971, pp. 234-45.

Sen Gupta, S. C., "Pastoral Romance and Romantic Comedy: *Rosalynde* and *As You Like It*," in *A Shakespeare Manual*, Oxford University Press, 1977, pp. 69-84.

Shakespeare, William, *As You Like It*, edited by Albert Gilman, New American Library, 1986.

——————, *The Complete Illustrated Shakespeare*, edited by Howard Staunton, reprint,

Park Lane, 1979.

Shaw, John, "Fortune and Nature in *As You Like It*," in *Shakespeare Quarterly*, Vol. 6, No. 1, 1955, pp. 45-50.

Spurgeon, Caroline F. E., "Imagery Establishes Atmosphere and Background in the Comedies," in *Readings on the Comedies*, edited by Clarice Swisher, Greenhaven Press, 1997, pp. 62-71.

Stauffer, Donald A., "The Garden of Eden," in *Shakespeare's World of Images: The Development of Moral Ideas*, Norton, 1949, pp. 67-109.

Van Doren, Mark, "*As You Like It*," in Shakespeare, Holt, 1939, pp. 151-60.

Wain, John, "Laughter and Judgement," in *The Living World of Shakespeare: A Playgoer's Guide*, St. Martin's, 1964, pp. 73-103.

Further Reading

Carroll, William C., *The Metamorphoses of Shakespearean Comedy*, Princeton University Press, 1985.

> Carroll provides a comprehensive analysis of the various personal transformations that the characters in Shakespeare's comedies undergo.

Craun, Edwin David, *Lies, Slander and Obscenity in Medieval English Literature: Pastoral Rhetoric and the Deviant Speaker*, Cambridge University Press, 2005.

> In this academic volume, Craun explains how the work of authors writing centuries before Shakespeare was affected by the rising power and influence of Christianity and the medieval clergy. Touchstone's role in *As You Like It* gains considerable weight when read with this study in mind.

Scheese, Don, *Nature Writing: The Pastoral Impulse in America*, Twayne, 1996.

> After surveying the historical development of literary pastoral conventions, Scheese focuses on how attitudes about and references to nature, especially in opposition to

industrialization, have shaped the writings of certain Americans.

Young, David, *The Heart's Forest: A Study of Shakespeare's Pastoral Plays*, Yale University Press, 1972.

> Young examines the intersection of romance and nature in all of Shakespeare's plays featuring pastoral conventions.

Lightning Source UK Ltd.
Milton Keynes UK
UKHW020636120922
408721UK00009B/951